Football grounds

i-SPY

D1173664

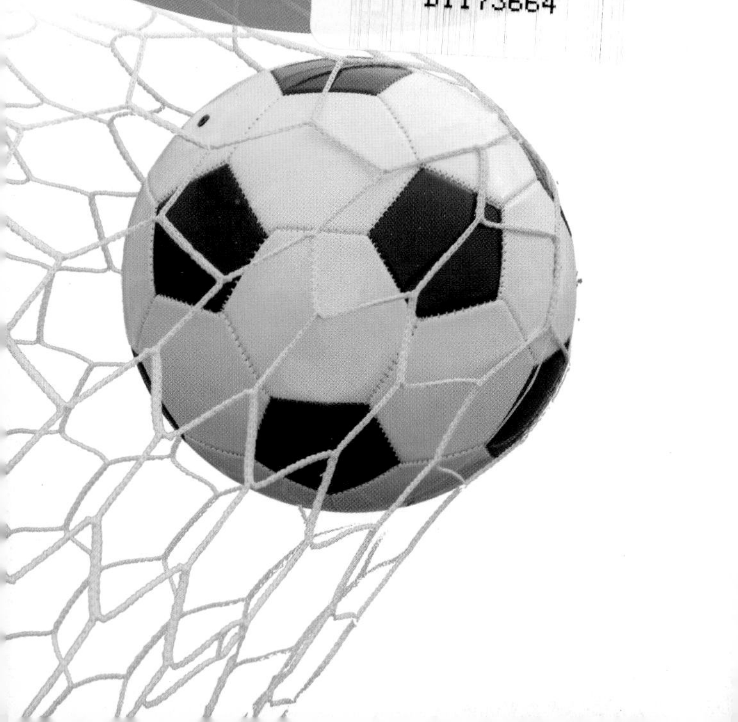

INTRODUCTION

Football is an institution in the UK. The first ever national competition played anywhere in the world was the FA Cup, which was first contested in the 1871–72 season, and the first ever league competition was the Football League which began in 1888–89 with 12 founder members. In Scotland the first FA Cup competition was held in 1873–74 and the Scottish League followed in 1890–91.

There are thousands of football clubs all over the country. This book gives you ground information and a small insight into the clubs which made up the Premier League and Football League in England during the 2015–16 season, plus the top clubs in Scotland, and the national stadia of England, Scotland and Wales.

In the early days, football grounds would have been mostly open terraces situated close to the pitch, with perhaps one small stand to accommodate seated spectators. This made for an exciting atmosphere when the grounds were full, and this characteristic of British football grounds is still envied all over the world.

More recently health and safety issues have had to be considered, and all clubs have had to upgrade their existing facilities or move to a new purpose-built ground. In fact, of the clubs listed in this book, around one third of them have moved home within the last 30 years. Note that the pitch sizes are approximate as they can be changed to suit the home team!

So start with your local club and get clocking up your i-SPY points now!

How to use your i-SPY book

The book is arranged in alphabetical order by the names of the football clubs, starting with those in England. Some grounds are not so easy to spot but even if you spot them on television you are entitled to half score. You need 1000 points to send off for your i-SPY certificate (see page 64) but that is not too difficult because there are masses of points in every book. Each entry has a star or circle and points value beside it. The stars represent harder to spot entries. As you make each i-SPY, write your score in the circle or star.

Points: 35 **Top Spot!**

ACCRINGTON STANLEY

Ground Name Wham Stadium/
Crown Ground
Capacity 5057 (2000 seated)
Address Livingstone Road,
Accrington, Lancashire, BB5 5BX
Pitch Size 101.5 x 66 m
Nickname The 'Owd Reds/Stanley
Year Founded 1968
Website www.accringtonstanley.co.uk

Accrington were one of the founder members of the Football League. Following their closure in 1893, a nearby team, Stanley Villa (named after their ground in Stanley Street), renamed themselves Accrington Stanley.

ARSENAL

Points: 5

Ground Name Emirates Stadium
Capacity 60 272 (all seated)
Address Hornsey Road, London, N7 7AJ
Pitch Size 105 x 68 m
Nickname The Gunners
Year Founded 1886 (originally Dial Square)
Website www.arsenal.com

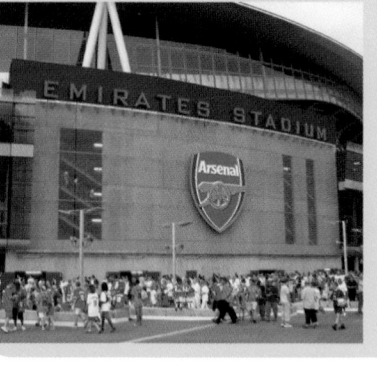

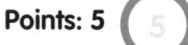

Starting life as Dial Square in Woolwich, southeast London, the club did not move north of the river until 1913. The local Underground station Gillespie Road was renamed after the club in 1932. Arsène Wenger is their longest ever serving manger (since October 1996). They moved to the Emirates Stadium when Highbury closed in 2006, after 93 years.

ASTON VILLA

Points: 10

Ground Name Villa Park
Capacity 42 640 (all seated)
Address Trinity Road, Birmingham, B6 6HE
Pitch Size 105 x 68 m
Nickname The Villa/The Villans/The Lions
Year Founded 1874
Website www.avfc.co.uk

Villa were founder members of the Football League and are one of the most successful clubs in English football, with seven League titles, seven FA Cups, five League Cups and one European Cup to their name. Villa Park has hosted 55 FA Cup semi-finals, more than any other club ground.

Points: 25

BARNET

Ground Name The Hive Stadium
Capacity 5176 (3434 seated)
Address Camrose Avenue, London, HA8 6AG
Pitch Size 106 x 70 m
Nickname The Bees
Year Founded 1888
Website www.barnetfc.com

When Barnet entered the Football League for the first time in 1991 their chairman was well-known ticket tout Stan Flashman and their manager was the colourful character Barry Fry. The relationship was fiery to say the least, and Stan used to sack Barry and then reinstate him at regular intervals!

BARNSLEY

Ground Name
Oakwell
Capacity 23 287
(all seated)
Address Grove
Street, Barnsley,
S71 1ET
Pitch Size 100.5 x 68.5 m
Nickname The Tykes/The Reds
Year Founded 1887 (originally
Barnsley St. Peter's)
Website www.barnsleyfc.co.uk

Barnsley were formed by a clergyman, Tiverton Preedy, in 1887, and have played more seasons in the second tier of English football than any other club. They reached the top division for the first time ever in 1997 but lasted just the one season in the Premier League.

POINTS: 20

BIRMINGHAM CITY

Ground Name
St Andrew's
Capacity 30 016
(all seated)
Address
St Andrews
Stadium,
Birmingham, B9 4RL
Pitch Size 100 x 66 m
Nickname The Blues
Year Founded 1875 (originally Small
Heath Alliance)
Website www.bcfc.com

Way before Manchester United and Liverpool, Birmingham City were the first English club in Europe when they competed in the Inter-Cities Fairs Cup in 1956. They were also the first to reach a European final in 1960 when they lost the Fairs Cup 4-1 on aggregate to Barcelona.

15 **Points: 15**

BLACKBURN ROVERS

Ground Name
Ewood Park
Capacity 31 367
(all seated)
Address
Blackburn,
Lancashire, BB2 4JF
Pitch Size 105 x 69 m
Nickname Rovers/Blue and Whites/
The Riversiders
Year Founded 1875
Website www.rovers.co.uk

Rovers are one of only three clubs to be founder members of both the Football League (1888) and the Premier League (1992). They are also one of the few clubs to have won the Premier League; this honour came in 1995 when they were owned by local businessman Jack Walker.

Points: 15

BLACKPOOL

Ground Name
Bloomfield Road
Capacity 17 338
(all seated)
Address
Seasiders Way,
Blackpool,
Lancashire, FY1 6JJ
Pitch Size 102 x 68 m
Nickname The Seasiders/
The Tangerines/The 'Pool
Year Founded 1887
Website www.blackpoolfc.co.uk

The Seasiders are easily identifiable as they are the only team in the league to wear tangerine shirts. Their finest hour was the 1953 FA Cup final when they recovered from 3-1 down to beat Bolton Wanderers 4-3. Stan Mortensen scored a hat-trick but the match is remembered for the performance of 38 year-old winger Stanley Matthews.

Points: 20

BOLTON WANDERERS

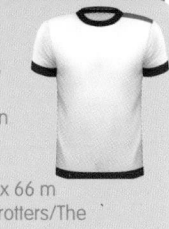

Ground Name Macron Stadium
Capacity 28 723 (all seated)
Address Burden Way, Horwich, Bolton, BL6 6JW
Pitch Size 100.5 x 66 m
Nickname The Trotters/The Wanderers
Year Founded 1874 (originally Christ Church FC)
Website www.bwfc.co.uk

Wanderers' greatest ever player was Nat Lofthouse who died in 2011. Born in the town, he scored 255 goals in 452 League appearances (as well as 30 goals for England in 33 matches), and after his playing career ended he also served as manager, chief scout, administrative manager, executive manager and president.

Points: 15

BOURNEMOUTH (AFC)

Ground Name Dean Court/ Vitality Stadium
Capacity 11 464 (all seated)
Address Kings Park, Bournemouth, Dorset, BH7 7AF
Pitch Size 105 x 78 m
Nickname The Cherries
Year Founded 1890 (originally Boscombe John's Institute)
Website www.afcb.co.uk

AFC Bournemouth is just the simplified trading name for the club which has been officially registered as Bournemouth and Boscombe Athletic since 1923. Their highest ever score came in 1971 in the FA Cup against Margate, when Ted MacDougall scored nine times in an 11-0 win.

Points: 15

BRADFORD CITY

Ground Name
Valley Parade/
Coral Windows
Stadium
Capacity 25 136
(all seated)
Address Bradford,
West Yorkshire, BD8 7DY
Pitch Size 103 x 64 m
Nickname The Bantams/The
Paraders/The Citizens
Year Founded 1903
Website www.bradfordcityfc.co.uk

The Bantams formed in 1903 and were immediately elected into Division Two despite never having played a game before. Valley Parade has been their only stadium, and sadly the ground is most famous for a fire on the last day of the 1984–85 season when 56 supporters lost their lives.

Points: 25

BRENTFORD

Ground Name
Griffin Park
Capacity 12 763
(all seated)
Address
Braemar Road,
Brentford, TW8 0NT
Pitch Size 100.5 x 67 m
Nickname The Bees, The Reds
Year Founded 1889
Website www.brentfordfc.co.uk

The Bees were a permanent fixture in Division One in their 1930s heyday – their best ever position was fifth in 1935–36. Their Griffin Park stadium was famous for being the only ground in English football with a pub at each corner, but one has now closed.

Points: 20

Points: 20

BRIGHTON AND HOVE ALBION

Ground Name Falmer Stadium/American Express Community Stadium
Capacity 30 750 (all seated)
Address Village Way, Falmer, Brighton, BN1 9BL
Pitch Size 105 x 69 m
Nickname The Seagulls/ The Albion
Year Founded 1901
Website www.seagulls. co.uk

The Seagulls left their Goldstone Ground stadium in 1997 and groundshared at Gillingham for two seasons, which is 73 miles away! They then moved to the Withdean which was an athletics stadium, as well as serving time as a zoo. The club moved to the purpose-built Falmer Stadium in 2011.

BRISTOL CITY

Points: 20

Ground Name Ashton Gate
Capacity 27 000 (all seated)
Address Ashton Road, Bristol, BS3 2EJ
Pitch Size 105 x 68.5 m
Nickname The Robins/The Reds/Cider Army
Year Founded 1897
Website www.bcfc.co.uk

Between 1980 and 1982 City became the first English team to suffer relegation three seasons in succession, dropping from the old First Division to the Fourth. To make matters worse the club was then declared bankrupt!

BRISTOL ROVERS

Ground Name Memorial Stadium
Capacity 11 916 (3 000 seated)
Address Filton Avenue, Horfield, Bristol, BS7 0BF
Pitch Size 101 x 68 m
Nickname The Pirates/The Gas
Year Founded 1883 (originally Black Arabs)
Website www.bristolrovers.co.uk

Rovers supporters are nicknamed the Gasheads, a derogatory term coined by Bristol City supporters referring to the large gasworks which was close to the Eastville Stadium where they played for most of their history.

BURNLEY

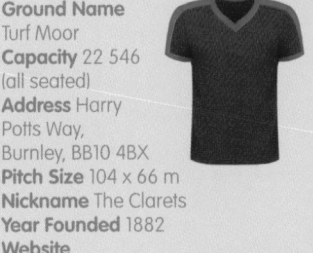

Ground Name Turf Moor
Capacity 22 546 (all seated)
Address Harry Potts Way, Burnley, BB10 4BX
Pitch Size 104 x 66 m
Nickname The Clarets
Year Founded 1882
Website www.burnleyfootballclub.com

Burnley were founder members of the Football League and are one of just three teams to have won all top four divisions. Back in 1910 they changed their colours from green to claret and blue to copy Aston Villa, who were the most successful team at that time.

 **Points: 35** Top Spot!

Points: 20

BURTON ALBION

Ground Name
Pirelli Stadium
Capacity 6912
(2034 seated)
Address Princess
Way, Burton-On-
Trent, DE13 0BH
Pitch Size 101 x 66 m
Nickname Brewers
Year Founded 1950
Website www.burtonalbionfc.co.uk

The Brewers were formed as recently as 1950 and reached the Football League in 2009. When they held Manchester United to a 0-0 draw at home in the FA Cup third round in 2006, Albion were backed in the replay by 11 000 supporters, the biggest away contingent ever seen at Old Trafford.

Points: 25

BURY

Ground Name
Gigg Lane
Capacity 11 840
(all seated)
Address Gigg Lane,
Bury, Lancashire,
BL9 9HR
Pitch Size 102.5 x 67 m
Nickname The Shakers
Year Founded 1885
Website www.buryfc.co.uk

Bury have won the FA Cup twice in 1900 and 1903 and achieved their highest league position of 4th in the then First Division in 1926. Their 6-0 victory over Derby County in the 1903 FA Cup is still the highest ever winning margin in a final.

Points: 25

CAMBRIDGE UNITED

Points: 30

Ground Name Abbey Stadium
Capacity 8127 (4376 seated)
Address Newmarket Road, Cambridge, CB5 8LN
Pitch Size 100.5 x 68 m
Nickname United/The Us
Year Founded 1912 (originally Abbey United)
Website www.cambridge-united.co.uk

The Us most successful period was in the early 1990s. In 1990 they became the first team from Division Four to reach the FA Cup quarter finals, and were promoted through the play-offs. The next year they won the Third Division and reached the FA Cup quarter-finals again. Then in 1992 they missed out in the play-offs to join the inaugural Premier League.

Points: 15

CARDIFF CITY

Ground Name Cardiff City Stadium
Capacity 33 280 (all seated)
Address Leckwith Road, Cardiff, CF11 8AZ
Pitch Size 100.5 x 68.5 m
Nickname The Bluebirds
Year Founded 1899 (originally Riverside AFC)
Website www.cardiffcityfc.co.uk

Cardiff are the only non-English club to ever win the FA Cup. They beat Arsenal 1-0 in the 1927 final, and the deciding goal was due to a mistake by the Gunners' keeper Dan Lewis, who just happened to be Welsh! Throughout their history, Cardiff have played most of their seasons in the second or third tier of English football, however 2012–13 saw them gain promotion to the Premier League and play in the top flight for the first time in 50 years.

CARLISLE UNITED

Ground Name Brunton Park
Capacity 18 202 (all seated)
Address Warwick Road, Carlisle, CA1 1LL
Pitch Size 102.5 x 67.5 m
Nickname The Cumbrians/The Blues/Blue and White Army
Year Founded 1904
Website www.carlisleunited.co.uk

Three straight wins at the start of 1974–75 saw Carlisle United sitting at the top of Division One. However they went on to finish bottom and that was their one and only season in the top flight. Severe flooding of the ground in the winters of 2005 and 2015 forced the team to play some home games at alternative grounds.

CHARLTON ATHLETIC

Ground Name The Valley
Capacity 27 111 (all seated)
Address Floyd Road, London, SE7 8BL
Pitch Size 102.5 x 67 m
Nickname The Addicks/Red Robins/The Valiants
Year Founded 1905
Website www.cafc.co.uk

Why are Charlton known as the Addicks? One theory is that it comes from the southeast London pronunciation of 'addock' (haddock) as used by a local fishmonger who used to serve the team with haddock and chips.

 **Points: 35** Top Spot!

15 **Points: 15**

13

CHELSEA

Points: 5

Ground Name Stamford Bridge
Capacity 41 663 (all seated)
Address Fulham Road, London, SW6 1HS
Pitch Size 103 x 67.5 m
Nickname The Blues, The Pensioners
Year Founded 1905
Website www.chelseafc.com

Chelsea have played at Stamford Bridge since their formation in 1905, but the stadium was in fact opened in 1877. For the first 28 years it was used by the London Athletic Club for athletics meetings and no football was played there at all. The turn of the century saw investment flood into Chelsea and with it success on the pitch as Chelsea won back-to-back championships in 2004–05 and 2005–06. Further domestic honours followed in the next decade and the club won the UEFA Champions League in 2011–12. This success has brought more fans to the club and plans to redevelop Stamford Bridge have regularly been considered in recent years.

CHESTERFIELD

Ground Name
Proact Stadium
Capacity 10 504
(all seated)
Address 1866
Sheffield Road,
Whittington Moor,
Chesterfield,
S41 8NZ
Pitch Size 101.5 x 65 m
Nickname The Spireites
Year Founded 1867
Website www.chesterfield-fc.co.uk

Although the exact date is uncertain, it is thought that Chesterfield were formed back in 1867 by members of a cricket club who needed to amuse themselves during the winter months. Their nickname is in honour of the town's most famous landmark, the crooked spire at the top of its 14th century church.

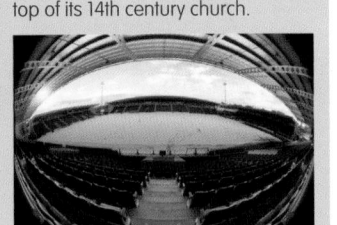

COLCHESTER UNITED

Ground Name
Weston Homes
Community
Stadium
Capacity 10 105
(all seated)
Address United
Way, Colchester,
CO4 5UP
Pitch Size 100.5 x 64 m
Nickname The Us
Year Founded 1937
Website www.cu-fc.com

Colchester are most famous for creating one of the biggest shocks in FA Cup history. As a Fourth Division club they beat the then mighty Leeds United 3-2 in the fifth round in 1971 with goals from former England international Ray Crawford (2) and David Simmons.

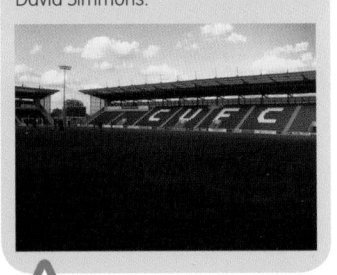

 **Points: 25**

☆ **Points: 30**

COVENTRY CITY

Points: 25

Ground Name Ricoh Arena
Capacity 32 609 (all seated)
Address 71 Phoenix Way, Foleshill, Coventry, CV6 6GE
Pitch Size 105 x 68 m
Nickname The Sky Blues
Year Founded 1883 (originally Singers)
Website www.ccfc.co.uk

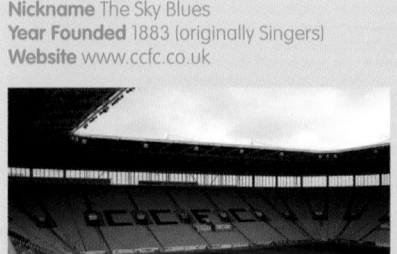

The club was formed by workers at Singer's cycle factory in 1883. Until the move to the Ricoh Arena in 2005, Highfield Road had been their home for more than a century. In 1981 it was converted to become the first English all-seater stadium.

Points: 35 **Top Spot!**

CRAWLEY TOWN

Ground Name Broadfield Stadium/Checkatrade.com Stadium
Capacity 6134 (3295 seated)
Address Winfield Way, Broadfield, Crawley, RH11 9RX
Pitch Size 100.5 x 68.5 m
Nickname Red Devils/The Reds
Year Founded 1896
Website www.crawleytownfc.com

In winning the 2010–11 Blue Square Premier to take their place in the Football League, Crawley reached a record points total of 105 and also set a new milestone by going 30 matches unbeaten up to the end of the season.

CREWE ALEXANDRA

Ground Name Alexandra Stadium
Capacity 10 153 (all seated)
Address Gresty Road, Crewe, Cheshire, CW2 6EB
Pitch Size 91.5 x 66.5 m
Nickname The Railwaymen/The Alex
Year Founded 1877 (originally Crewe)
Website www.crewealex.net

The club is said to be named after Princess Alexandra of Denmark, the wife of Edward VII. In the mid-1950s Crewe put together a sequence of 56 away matches without a win! They have also finished bottom of the Football League on eight occasions, more than any other club.

CRYSTAL PALACE

Ground Name Selhurst Park
Capacity 26 309 (all seated)
Address Selhurst Park, London, SE25 6PU
Pitch Size 100.5 x 67.5 m
Nickname The Eagles/The Glaziers
Year Founded 1905
Website www.cpfc.co.uk

The Eagles reached the FA Cup final in 1990 for the first and only time, where they met Manchester United. As this was the first ever 3-3 draw in the final they can claim to have made history. Gary O'Reilly and Ian Wright (2) were the Palace scorers. United won the replay 1-0 five days later.

 **Points: 25**

Points: 10

DAGENHAM & REDBRIDGE

Top Spot! Points: 35

35

Ground Name Victoria Road
Capacity 6078 (all seated)
Address Dagenham, Essex, RM10 7XL
Pitch Size 102.5 x 66 m
Nickname The Daggers/Dag & Red
Year Founded 1992
Website www.daggers.co.uk

In 1979 Leytonstone merged with Ilford. In 1988 Leytonstone-Ilford merged with Walthamstow Avenue to become Redbridge Forest. In 1992 Redbridge Forest merged with Dagenham to give us Dagenham & Redbridge. Simple really!

Points: 20

20

DERBY COUNTY

Ground Name Pride Park Stadium/iPro Stadium
Capacity 33 597 (all seated)
Address Derby, DE24 8XL
Pitch Size 105 x 67.5 m
Nickname The Rams
Year Founded 1884
Website www.dcfc.co.uk

Derby County won the League in 1972 managed by the great Brian Clough and assisted by Peter Taylor. The Rams also won the League in 1975. They are the only club to have hosted full England internationals at three home grounds: in 1895 at the Racecourse Ground, in 1911 at the Baseball Ground and finally in 2001 at Pride Park.

DONCASTER ROVERS

Points: 25

25

Ground Name Keepmoat Stadium
Capacity 15 231 (all seated)
Address Stadium Way, Lakeside, Doncaster, DN4 5JW
Pitch Size 99.5 x 69.5 m
Nickname The Rovers/Donny/ The Vikings
Year Founded 1879
Website www.doncasterroversfc.co.uk

In 1946 Rovers played Stockport County away in a Division Three (North) cup tie which became the longest ever football match. With the aggregate scores level after 90 minutes, it was decided that play would continue until one team scored. After 203 minutes, with darkness closing in, the game had to be stopped. There are stories of fans going home for their tea, then coming back to watch the end of the game! The replay at Doncaster was won by Rovers 4-0.

EVERTON

10 **Points: 10**

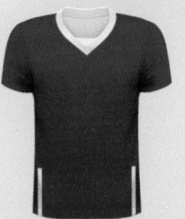

Ground Name Goodison Park
Capacity 39 572 (all seated)
Address Goodison Road, Liverpool, L4 4EL
Pitch Size 100.5 x 68 m
Nickname The Toffees/The Blues
Year Founded 1878 (originally St Domingo's)
Website www.evertonfc.com

The most famous player in the club's history is Dixie Dean. When Everton won the Football League in 1927–28 he scored 60 goals, a feat never achieved before or since. He scored 383 times in 433 appearances for the Toffees, including 37 hat-tricks. A statue of Dixie stands outside the Park End of Goodison Park bearing the inscription 'Footballer, Gentleman, Evertonian'.

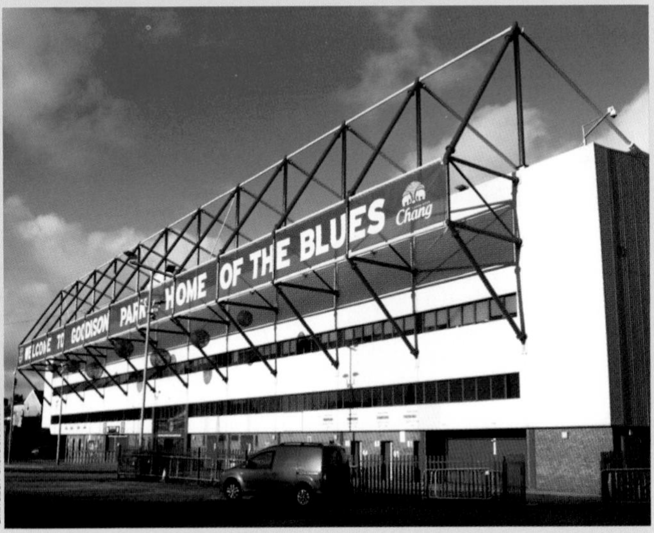

amirraizat / Shutterstock.com

EXETER CITY

Ground Name
St James Park
Capacity 8541
(3000 seated)
Address Stadium
Way, Exeter,
Devon, EX4 6PX
Pitch Size 104 x
66.5 m
Nickname The Grecians
Year Founded 1904
Website www.exetercityfc.co.uk

The Grecians went on a historic tour of South America in 1914, and it is believed that the Brazilian national team played its first ever match against City. According to different sources the game ended in a 2-0 win for Brazil, or it might have been a 3-3 draw...!

 **Points: 30**

FLEETWOOD TOWN

Ground Name
Highbury Stadium
Capacity 5327
(2701 seats)
Address Park
Ave, Fleetwood,
Lancashire FY7 6SP
Pitch Size 103 x
68 m
Nickname Cod Army
Year Founded 1908
Website
www.fleetwoodtownfc.com

Fleetwood Town's origins date back to 1908 but the current club was properly established in 1997. They gained promotion from non-league football in 2011–12 and played their first season in the Football League in 2012–13. After two strong seasons they won the play-off final of 2013–14 to gain promotion to League One for the first time in their history.

Points: 45 Top Spot!

FULHAM

Ground Name Craven Cottage
Capacity 25 700 (plans to expand to 30 000) (all seated)
Address Stevenage Road, London, SW6 6HH
Pitch Size 100.5 x 68.5 m
Nickname The Cottagers/The Whites/The Lilywhites
Year Founded 1879 (originally Fulham St Andrew's Church Sunday School)
Website www.fulhamfc.com

Fulham's stadium is an architect's delight. The Cottage Pavilion was built in 1905 and can still be seen in one corner of the ground. Both this and the Johnny Haynes Stand (named after their most famous player) are designated Grade II listed buildings.

Points: 15

GILLINGHAM

Ground Name MEMS Priestfield Stadium
Capacity 11 582 (all seated)
Address Redfern Avenue, Gillingham, Kent, ME7 4DD
Pitch Size 104 x 68.5 m
Nickname The Gills
Year Founded 1893 (originally New Brompton)
Website www.gillinghamfootballclub.com

The Gills are the only Football League club based in Kent. When Tony Cascarino was signed from Kent League team Crockenhill in 1982 the transfer fee they paid was reportedly a new set of tracksuits!

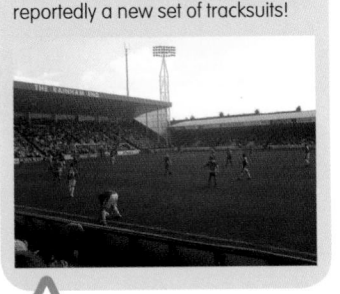

Points: 25

HARTLEPOOL UNITED

40

Ground Name Victoria Park
Capacity 7 856 (4 402 seated)
Address Clarence Road, Hartlepool, TS24 8BZ
Pitch Size 103 x 70.5 m
Nickname The 'Pool/Monkey Hangers
Year Founded 1908 (originally Hartlepools United)
Website www.hartlepoolunited.co.uk

The club's nickname derives from the Napoleonic Wars when a French ship was wrecked off the coast of the town. The only survivor was a monkey who was brought to trial on suspicion of being a spy. As he was unable to answer the questions he was hanged anyway!

Points: 25

25

HUDDERSFIELD TOWN

Ground Name John Smith's Stadium
Capacity 24 500 (all seated)
Address Stadium Way, Huddersfield, HD1 6PX
Pitch Size 105 x 69.5 m
Nickname The Terriers
Year Founded 1908
Website www.htafc.com

The glory days for the Terriers were way back in the 1920s. In 1926 they became the first club to win three successive League titles and were then runners-up for the next two seasons. They also won the FA Cup in 1922 and were losing finalists in 1920 and 1928.

HULL CITY

Points: 20

20

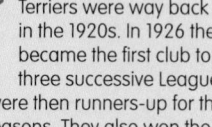

Ground Name KC Stadium
Capacity 25 586 (all seated)
Address West Park, Hull, HU3 6HU
Pitch Size 114 x 74 m
Nickname The Tigers
Year Founded 1904
Website www.hullcitytigers.com

Until the Tigers were promoted to the Premier League in 2008, Hull was widely held to be the largest city in Europe never to have had a football team in the top division of their national league. Their greatest triumph was reaching the 2014 FA Cup final where they lost to Arsenal 3-2.

IPSWICH TOWN

Ground Name Portman Road
Capacity 30 311 (all seated)
Address Portman Road, Ipswich, IP1 2DA
Pitch Size 102 x 75 m
Nickname The Blues/Town/The Tractor Boys/Pride of East Anglia
Year Founded 1878
Website www.itfc.co.uk

In 1961 Ipswich won the Football League with Alf Ramsey as manager. In 1978 they won the FA Cup with Bobby Robson as manager. Both moved on to manage the England team, Ramsey guiding them to the 1966 World Cup victory and Robson taking England to the World Cup semi-finals in 1990.

Points: 20

LEEDS UNITED

Ground Name Elland Road
Capacity 37 914 (all seated)
Address Elland Road, Leeds, LS11 0ES
Pitch Size 105 x 68 m
Nickname United/The Whites/The Peacocks
Year Founded 1919
Website www.leedsunited.com

When Don Revie became manager of Leeds in 1961 he changed their kit to all-white to emulate the mighty Real Madrid. It seemed to do the trick as under his stewardship they won the League three times, were runners-up five times, and won the FA Cup for the only time in their history in 1972.

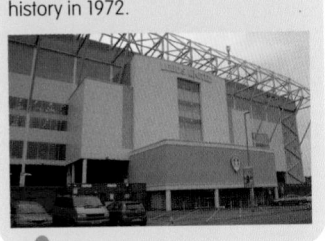

Points: 20

Points: 10

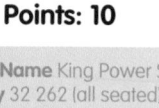 **LEICESTER CITY**

Ground Name King Power Stadium
Capacity 32 262 (all seated)
Address Filbert Way, Leicester, LE2 7FL
Pitch Size 102 x 67 m
Nickname The Foxes
Year Founded 1884 (originally Leicester Fosse)
Website www.lcfc.com

The club's original name referred to Fosse Road, which was close to their ground. In 1891 they moved to Filbert Street and stayed there until 2002. After two decades of regular promotion and relegation, the fantastic 2015–16 campaign looks to have established them in the top flight for years to come.

LEYTON ORIENT

Points: 30

Ground Name Brisbane Road/Matchroom Stadium
Capacity 9271 (all seated)
Address Oliver Road, Leyton, London, E10 5NF
Pitch Size 105 x 73 m
Nickname The Os/Orient
Year Founded 1881 (originally Eagle Cricket Club)
Website www.leytonorient.com

For the last match of the 1914–15 season Clapton Orient drew a crowd of over 20 000. They were there to pay tribute to the club because 41 of its players and staff had joined the 17th Battalion Middlesex Regiment to serve in the First World War, the highest number from any football club.

5

Points: 5

LIVERPOOL

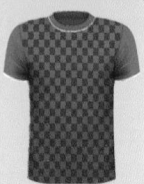

Ground Name Anfield
Capacity 45 522 (all seated) with plans to expand to 50 000
Address Anfield Road, Liverpool, L4 0TH
Pitch Size 100.5 x 68 m
Nickname The Reds
Year Founded 1892
Website www.liverpoolfc.com

If there had not been a dispute between Everton and their landlord at Anfield, John Houlding, Liverpool FC might never have formed. In 1892 Everton moved to Goodison Park and Mr Houlding founded a new club to play on the Anfield site. The rest is history…

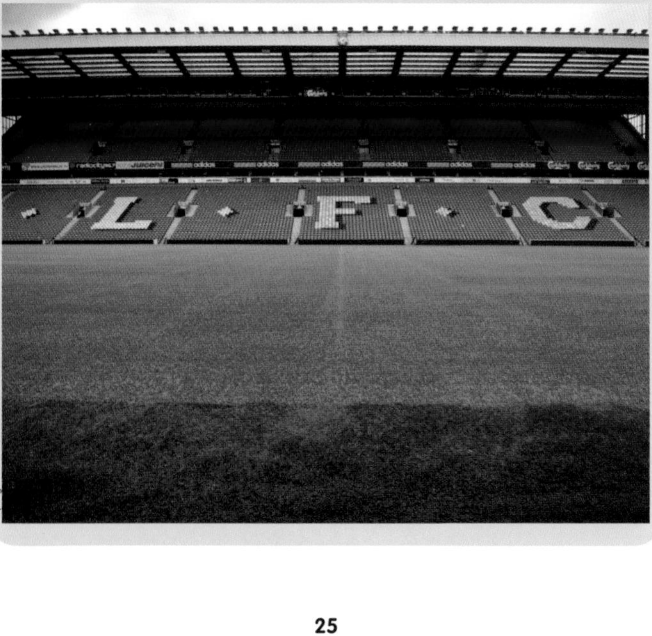

naipung / shutterstock.com

Points: 35   **Top Spot!**

LUTON TOWN

Ground Name Kenilworth Road
Capacity 10 356 (all seated)
Address 1 Maple Road, Luton, LU4 8AW
Pitch Size 100.5 x 66 m
Nickname The Hatters
Year Founded 1885
Website www.lutontown.co.uk

Luton were the first club in the south of England to turn professional, in 1891. On 13 April 1936 Joe Payne scored 10 goals for the Hatters in a 12-0 win against Bristol Rovers; this is still a record for the Football League.

MANCHESTER CITY

Points: 10

Ground Name City of Manchester Stadium/Etihad Stadium
Capacity 55 097 (all seated)
Address Etihad Campus, Manchester, M11 3FF
Pitch Size 105 x 67.5 m
Nickname The Sky Blues/The Citizens/City
Year Founded 1880 (originally St Mark's (West Gorton))
Website www.mcfc.co.uk

City's home from 1923 to 2003 was Maine Road, and initially the club was hoping to have a stadium with a capacity of 120 000! Nevertheless the crowd of 84 569 for an FA Cup tie with Stoke City in 1934 remains the highest ever attendance for an English club ground. Investment into the club in 2008 led to City becoming one of the wealthiest clubs in world football.

Points: 5

MANCHESTER UNITED

Ground Name Old Trafford
Capacity 75 653 (all seated)
Address Sir Matt Busby Way, Manchester, M16 0RA
Pitch Size 105 x 68 m
Nickname The Red Devils
Year Founded 1878 (originally Newton Heath)
Website www.manutd.com

When United became the first English winners of the European Cup by beating Benfica 4-1 at Wembley in 1968, their team contained three European Footballers of the Year: Bobby Charlton, Denis Law and George Best, who are immortalised in a statue outside Old Trafford.

Debu55y / shutterstock.com

MANSFIELD TOWN

Ground Name Field Mill/One Call Stadium
Capacity 9 186
Address Quarry Lane, Mansfield, Nottinghamshire, NG18 5DA
Pitch Size 104 x 64 m
Nickname The Stags/Yellows
Year Founded 1897 (originally Mansfield Wesleyans)
Website www.mansfieldtown.net

The Stags' greatest period of success was during the 1920s when they were a Midland League club, but six applications to join the Football League were rejected. In 1931 the club changed tactics and applied to the southern section of Division Three. This did the trick and they were voted in at Newport County's expense.

MIDDLESBROUGH

Ground Name Riverside Stadium
Capacity 34 742 (all seated)
Address Middlesbrough, Cleveland, TS3 6RS
Pitch Size 105 x 68.5 m
Nickname The Boro/The Smoggies/The Red Army
Year Founded 1876
Website www.mfc.co.uk

The history of big transfers starts here! When Middlesbrough signed Alf Common from Sunderland in February 1905 they paid a world record fee of £1000. In his first match Alf scored the only goal at Sheffield United to give Boro their first away win in nearly two years.

35 **Points: 35 Top Spot!**

15 **Points: 15**

MILLWALL

Ground Name
The Den
Capacity 20 146
(all seated)
Address Zampa
Road, London,
SE16 3LN
Pitch Size 105 x
68 m
Nickname The Lions
Year Founded 1885 (originally
Millwall Rovers)
Website www.millwallfc.co.uk

The original Millwall Rovers were formed by workers from a canning and preserving factory on the Isle of Dogs. The Lions can claim to have hosted the first ever League match to be played on a Sunday, against Fulham in 1974.

Points: 25

MILTON KEYNES DONS

Ground Name
Stadium mk
Capacity 30 700
(all seated)
Address Stadium
Way West, Milton
Keynes, MK1 1ST
Pitch Size 105
x 68 m
Nickname The Dons
Year Founded 2004
Website www.mkdons.com

MK Dons were formed as a result of Wimbledon FC's relocation to the National Hockey Stadium in Milton Keynes. The club originally claimed the history of Wimbledon as its own but now regards itself as an entirely new club.

Points: 25

Points: 45 — Top Spot!

MORECAMBE

Ground Name Globe Arena
Capacity 6476 (2247 seated)
Address Christie Way, Westgate, Morecambe, LA4 4TB
Pitch Size 100.5 x 69.5 m
Nickname The Shrimps/The Erics/Seasiders
Year Founded 1920
Website www.morecambefc.com

The club's benefactor in its early years was businessman J. B. Christie, who moved to the town when he retired. He helped arrange the lease of the original ground, which was renamed Christie Park in his honour, and his name lives on to this day at the Globe Arena which is on Christie Way.

NEWCASTLE UNITED

Points: 10

Ground Name St James' Park
Capacity 52 404 (all seated)
Address St James' Park, Newcastle-upon-Tyne, NE1 4ST
Pitch Size 105 x 68 m
Nickname The Magpies/The Toon/Geordies
Year Founded 1892
Website www.nufc.co.uk

It's true to say that the Toon Army have been starved of success when you consider that the club's most successful spell was over a century ago. Between 1904 and 1911 The Magpies won the League three times, the FA Cup once, and were beaten finalists four times.

NEWPORT COUNTY

Ground Name Rodney Parade
Capacity 7850
Address Rodney Parade, Newport, South Wales, NP19 0UU
Pitch Size 102.5 x 66 m
Nickname The Exiles, The Ironsides, The Port, The County
Year Formed 1912
Website www.newport-county.co.uk

Newport County is the professional football club based in Newport, South Wales. The club has spent much of its history in the lower leagues of the English Football League, although they did drop out of the league altogether in 1988. The club subsequently went bankrupt in 1989 before being reformed and starting a 20-year campaign back to the league ranks, returning for the 2013–14 season. In the 1980–81 season they achieved one of their major historical highlights by getting to the quarter-finals of the UEFA Cup Winner's Cup, before being defeated in two legs by then East German side Jena.

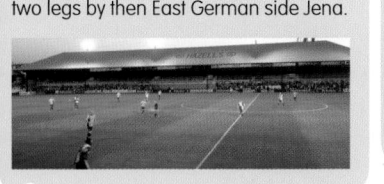

NORTHAMPTON TOWN

Ground Name Sixfields Stadium
Capacity 5000 – due to redevelopment (all seated)
Address Northampton, NN5 5QA
Pitch Size 106 x 66 m
Nickname The Cobblers/Tayn/Shoe Army
Year Founded 1897
Website www.ntfc.co.uk

The Cobblers have played just one season in the top flight, back in 1965–66. They had risen from the Fourth Division in just five years, but after one taste of the big time their fall was even quicker, and they were back in the Fourth Division again by 1969.

Points: 45 Top Spot!

Points: 40
Top Spot!

NORWICH CITY

Ground Name
Carrow Road
Capacity 27 244
(all seated)
Address Carrow
Road, Norwich,
NR1 1JE
Pitch Size 104 x
67.5 m
Nickname The Canaries
Year Founded 1902
Website www.canaries.co.uk

TV cook Delia Smith and her husband are joint majority shareholders of the club, and actor/comedian/author Stephen Fry is also a director. The fans' song 'On the Ball, City' is thought to be the world's oldest football song still in use. The Canaries are the only British side to have beaten Bayern Munich in their Olympic Stadium – which they did in the 1993–4 UEFA Cup.

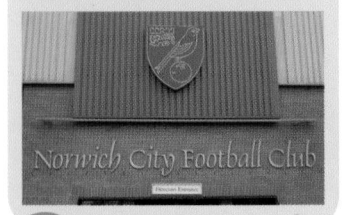

15 **Points: 15**

NOTTINGHAM FOREST

Ground Name
City Ground
Capacity 30 445
(all seated)
Address
Nottingham,
NG2 5FJ
Pitch Size 105 x 71 m
Nickname The Reds/Forest/The Tricky Trees
Year Founded 1865
Website www.nottinghamforest.co.uk

When Brian Clough took over as manager in 1975, along with Peter Taylor as his assistant, the club was in Division Two. Promoted in 1977, they then won the League title at the first attempt. More was to follow – Forest beat Malmö 1-0 to take the European Cup in 1979, and they retained it by beating Hamburg (with Kevin Keegan who had signed from Liverpool) 1-0 a year later.

20 **Points: 20**

NOTTS COUNTY

Ground Name
Meadow Lane
Capacity 19 588
(all seated)
Address
Meadow Lane,
Nottingham,
NG2 3HJ
Pitch Size 104 x 69.5 m
Nickname The Magpies
Year Founded 1862
Website www.nottscountyfc.co.uk

The Magpies were formed in 1862 and are the oldest existing professional football club in the world. They have been promoted 13 times and relegated 16 times in their history. Did you know that Juventus' black and white striped shirts are based on the Notts County kit?

OLDHAM ATHLETIC

Ground Name
Boundary Park/
SportsDirect.com
Park
Capacity 13 309
(all seated)
Address Oldham,
OL1 2PA
Pitch Size 100.5 x 67.5 m
Nickname The Latics
Year Founded 1895 (originally
Pine Villa)
Website www.oldhamathletic.co.uk

Oldham's place in the record books is one they would rather not have! On Boxing Day 1935 they suffered their record defeat, 13-4 at the hands of Tranmere Rovers. This is the game with the most goals ever in Football League history.

35 **Points: 35** **Top Spot!**

25 **Points: 25**

OXFORD UNITED

Ground Name
Kassam Stadium
Capacity 12 500
(all seated)
Address
Grenoble Road,
Oxford, OX4 4XP
Pitch Size 102.5 x
71 m
Nickname The Us/Yellows
Year Founded 1893 (originally
Headington United)
Website www.oufc.co.uk

In 1950 Headington United were
the first professional club in England
to install floodlights. At the time
they were playing in the Southern
League. The name change to Oxford
United in 1960 was intended to give
the club a bigger profile and they
were duly elected to the Football
League two years later.

 **Points: 30**

PETERBOROUGH UNITED

Ground Name
London Road
Stadium/ABAX
Stadium
Capacity 15 314
(all seated)
Address
London Road,
Peterborough, PE2 8AL
Pitch Size 102.5 x 69.5 m
Nickname The Posh
Year Founded 1934
Website www.theposh.com

In 1921 the manager of Fletton
United, forerunners of the current
club, said he was looking for 'posh
players for a posh new team' –
and so they became 'The Posh'.
Peterborough hold the record for
most goals scored in an English
season, 134 in Division Four in
1960–61.

Points: 30

PLYMOUTH ARGYLE

Ground Name Home Park
Capacity 17 800 (all seated)
Address Plymouth, PL2 3DQ
Pitch Size 104 x 71 m
Nickname The Pilgrims/The Greens/Argyle/The Green Army
Year Founded 1886 (originally Argyle)
Website www.pafc.co.uk

One of the most memorable days in the club's history was in 1973 when they staged a friendly against Brazilian club Santos. Playing for Santos was Pelé, possibly the greatest player in the history of the game. This didn't matter to Third Division Argyle who pulled off a shock 3-2 win!

Points: 30

PORT VALE

Ground Name Vale Park
Capacity 19 052 (all seated)
Address Hamil Road, Burslem, Stoke-on-Trent, ST6 1AW
Pitch Size 104 x 70.5 m
Nickname The Valiants/The Vale
Year Founded 1876
Website www.port-vale.co.uk

Port Vale is one of the few English League clubs whose name doesn't refer to a town or city. Instead, it reflects the place where the very first club meeting took place -— Port Vale House. Port Vale is actually the name of a valley of ports on the Trent and Mersey Canal. The club's most famous supporter is singer Robbie Williams and another big fan is darts legend Phil 'The Power' Taylor.

Points: 25

PORTSMOUTH

Ground Name
Fratton Park
Capacity
18 524 – due to
redevelopment.
(all seated)
Address
Frogmore Road,
Portsmouth, PO4 8RA
Pitch Size 105 x 66.5 m
Nickname Pompey/Blue Army
Year Founded 1898
Website www.portsmouthfc.co.uk

Pompey won the FA Cup final in 1939, beating Wolves 4-1. With World War II intervening, the next final was in 1946 so they retained the Cup for seven years. They won it again in 2008 when Kanu's goal was enough to defeat Cardiff City.

Points: 30

PRESTON NORTH END

Ground Name
Deepdale
Capacity 23 404
(all seated)
Address Sir Tom
Finney Way,
Preston, PR1 6RU
Pitch Size 100.5 x
68.5 m
Nickname The Lilywhites/North End/
The Whites/The Invincibles
Year Founded 1880
Website www.pnefc.net

Preston were the first champions of the Football League in 1888–89 and they also won the FA Cup the same year to complete the 'Double'. Their greatest ever player was Sir Tom Finney who scored 187 goals between 1946 and 1960 and has a stand at Deepdale named after him.

Points: 20

QUEENS PARK RANGERS

Ground Name
Loftus Road
Stadium
Capacity 18 439
(all seated)
Address South
Africa Road,
London, W12 7PJ
Pitch Size 102.5 x 66 m
Nickname QPR/Rangers/
The Hoops/The Rs
Year Founded 1882 (originally St Jude's)
Website www.qpr.co.uk

QPR hold the record for the most home grounds in the history of the Football League – 14! Their one major honour came in 1967 when as a Third Division club they won the League Cup against West Bromwich Albion, coming back from 2-0 down in the last half hour to win 3-2.

Points: 15

READING

Ground Name
Madejski Stadium
Capacity 24 161
(all seated)
Address
Junction 11, M4,
Reading, RG2 0FL
Pitch Size 105 x 68 m
Nickname The Royals
Year Founded 1871
Website www.readingfc.co.uk

Reading were originally nicknamed the Biscuitmen after one of the main trades in the town, Huntley & Palmers biscuits, but changed to the Royals when the factory closed down in 1970. The Royals biggest win was 10-2 against Crystal Palace in 1956 but their biggest defeat was 18-0 against Preston North End in 1894.

Points: 20

ROCHDALE

Ground Name Spotland Stadium
Capacity 10 249 (all seated)
Address Sandy Lane, Rochdale, OL11 5DR
Pitch Size 104 x 69.5 m
Nickname The Dale
Year Founded 1907
Website www.rochdalefc.co.uk

Rochdale has spent most of its Football League tenure in the lowest of the English professional leagues. They are notable however, for being one of only two clubs to play in the League Cup final while residing in the lowest league in 1962, although they did lose to Norwich City in the final 4-0 on aggregate.

 Points: 30

ROTHERHAM UNITED

Ground Name AESSEAL New York Stadium
Capacity 12 021 (all seated)
Address New York Way, Rotherham, S60 1AH
Pitch Size 100.5 x 66 m
Nickname The Millers
Year Founded 1925 (originally Thornhill)
Website www.themillers.co.uk

Rotherham's one and only major final appearance was in 1961, the first season that the League Cup competition was contested. The Millers beat Aston Villa 2-0 at home in the first leg but lost on aggregate after a 3-0 defeat at Villa Park.

Points: 30

SCUNTHORPE UNITED

Ground Name
Glanford Park
Capacity 9088
(all seated)
Address Jack
Brownsword
Way, Scunthorpe,
DN15 8TD
Pitch Size 102.5 x 66 m
Nickname The Iron
Year Founded 1899
Website www.scunthorpe-united.
co.uk

When Scunthorpe moved to Glanford Park in 1988 they were the first club since the 1950s to move to a brand new purpose-built stadium. Two of their best known players, Kevin Keegan and Ray Clemence, went on to fame and international honours in the great Liverpool team of the 1970s.

SHEFFIELD UNITED

Ground Name
Bramall Lane
Capacity 32 702
(all seated)
Address Bramall
Lane, Sheffield,
S2 4SU
Pitch Size 102.5 x
66 m
Nickname The Blades/Red and
White Wizards
Year Founded 1889
Website www.sufc.co.uk

In 1889 an FA Cup semi-final between Preston North End and West Bromwich Albion at Bramall Lane attracted a crowd of almost 23 000. The president of the cricket club that owned the ground saw the commercial possibilities and formed the football club six days later!

Points: 30

Points: 35   **Top Spot!**

SHEFFIELD WEDNESDAY

Ground Name
Hillsborough
Stadium
Capacity 39 812
(all seated)
Address
Sheffield, S6 1SW
Pitch Size 106 x
65 m
Nickname The Owls/SWFC/The
Wednesday
Year Founded 1867 (Originally The
Wednesday)
Website www.swfc.co.uk

When Wednesday reached the FA
Cup final in 1966 they were drawn
away from home in every round.
Given the option to wear their home
kit at Wembley, they chose to stick
with the lucky away strip. But the
luck ran out as Everton came from
2-0 down to beat the Owls 3-2.

Sheffield Wednesday – Hillsborough

Points: 25

SHREWSBURY TOWN

Ground Name
Greenhous
Meadow/New
Meadow
Capacity 9 875
(all seated)
Address
Oteley Road,
Shrewsbury,
SY2 6ST
Pitch Size 110 x 75 m
Nickname The Shrews/Salop/The
Blues/The Town
Year Founded 1886
Website www.shrewsburytown.com

The Shrews' ground for nearly a
century was Gay Meadow, situated
on the banks of the River Severn. For
many years a local coracle (boat)
maker provided an unusual service:
he would sit in his coracle during
home matches and retrieve any
stray footballs which found their way
into the river!

Points: 35 **Top Spot!**

Points: 10

SOUTHAMPTON

SOUTHAMPTON

Ground Name St. Mary's Stadium
Capacity 32 689 (all seated)
Address Britannia Road, Southampton, SO14 5FP
Pitch Size 102 x 68 m
Nickname The Saints
Year Founded 1885 (originally St. Mary's Y.M.A.)
Website www.saintsfc.co.uk

Centre-half Chris Nicholl made over 600 League appearances for various clubs, but his most memorable was in the colours of Southampton in 1976. Playing against Leicester City in a Division One match, Chris scored all four goals in a 2-2 draw!

SOUTHEND UNITED

Ground Name
Roots Hall
Capacity 12 392
(all seated)
Address
Victoria Avenue,
Southend-on-Sea,
SS2 6NQ
Pitch Size 100.5 x 67.5 m
Nickname The Shrimpers/The
Seasiders/The Blues
Year Founded 1906
Website www.southendunited.co.uk

The club moved to Roots Hall
in 1955, but construction of the
stadium was not completed
for another 11 years. Roots Hall
remained the newest ground in
the League right up to 1988, when
Scunthorpe moved to Glanford Park.

Points: 30

STEVENAGE

Ground Name
The Lamex
Stadium
Capacity 6722
(3142 seated)
Address
Broadhall Way,
Stevenage,
SG2 8RH
Pitch Size 100.5 x 64 m
Nickname The Boro
Year Founded 1976
Website www.stevenagefc.com

Stevenage had their 15 minutes of
fame in 1998 when they drew 1-1 at
Broadhall Way with Newcastle in the
FA Cup fourth round, then narrowly
lost the replay 2-1 at St. James' Park.
In 2010–11, Stevenage's first season
in the Football League, the Magpies
visited again for a third round tie and
this time The Boro won 3-1, their first
victory against first-tier opposition.

Points: 45 **Top Spot!**

STOKE CITY

Ground Name Britannia Stadium
Capacity 27 902 (all seated)
Address Stanley Matthews Way, Stoke-on-Trent, ST4 4EG
Pitch Size 100 x 64 m
Nickname The Potters
Year Founded 1863 (originally Stoke Ramblers)
Website www.stokecityfc.com

Stoke's most famous son, Sir Stanley Matthews was playing for the Potters in Division One when he was 50! Their first appearance in the FA Cup final was not until 2011 when they lost 1-0 to Manchester City, 148 years after the club was formed.

SUNDERLAND

Ground Name Stadium of Light
Capacity 49 000 (all seated)
Address Stadium of Light, Sunderland, SR5 1SU
Pitch Size 105 x 68 m
Nickname The Black Cats/The Mackems/The Lads
Year Founded 1879 (originally Sunderland and District Teachers)
Website www.safc.com

Sunderland's last major honour was the FA Cup in 1973, when as a Second Division club they upset the odds by beating Leeds United 1-0. Manager Bob Stokoe's triumphant run on to the pitch at the end of the match is commemorated by a statue outside the Stadium of Light.

 Points: 15

15 **Points: 15**

Points: 15

Ground Name Liberty Stadium
Capacity 20 520 (all seated)
Address Morfa, Swansea, SA1 2FA
Pitch Size 104 x 68 m
Nickname The Swans/The Jacks
Year Founded 1912 (originally Swansea Town)
Website www.swanseacity.net

In 2011 the Swans became the first Welsh club to play in the Premier League. Their original home ground – the Vetch Field – was named after a type of bean that was grown on its surface at the time.

SWINDON TOWN

Points: 30

Ground Name The County Ground
Capacity 15 728 (all seated)
Address County Road, Swindon, SN1 2ED
Pitch Size 101 x 64 m
Nickname The Robins/Town
Year Founded 1879 (originally as Swindon AFC)
Website www.swindontownfc.co.uk

Like QPR, Swindon's one major honour came in the League Cup as a Third Division club. Two extra-time goals from Don Rogers saw them beat Arsenal 3-1 in the 1969 final. Playing at left-back was John Trollope who made 770 League appearances for the Robins, an all-time record for one club in English football.

Points: 10

TOTTENHAM HOTSPUR

Ground Name White Hart Lane
Capacity 36 240 (all seated)
Address Bill Nicholson Way, 748 High Road, Tottenham, London, N17 0AP
Pitch Size 100 x 67 m
Nickname Spurs/The Lilywhites
Year Founded 1882 (originally Hotspur)
Websitewww.tottenhamhotspur.com

Supporters' folklore has it that Spurs are successful when the year ends in '1'. They won the League in 1951 and 1961, and the FA Cup in 1901, 1921, 1961, 1981 and 1991. The first Cup triumph came when the club was in the Southern League, making Tottenham the only non-league club to win the FA Cup since the Football League was formed.

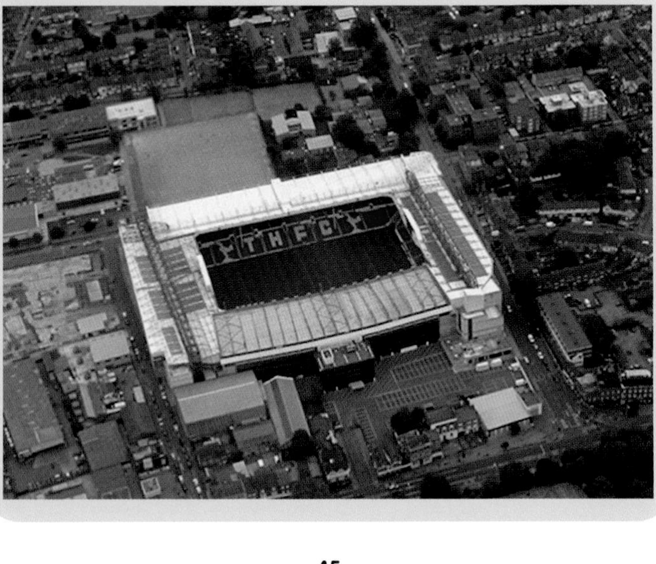

Points: 25

WALSALL

Ground Name Banks' Stadium/Bescot Stadium
Capacity 11 300 (all seated)
Address Bescot Crescent, Walsall, WS1 4SA
Pitch Size 100.5 x 66.5 m
Nickname The Saddlers
Year Founded 1888 (originally Walsall Town Swifts)
Website www.saddlers.co.uk

In 1933 Walsall beat Arsenal 2-0 in the FA Cup at Fellows Park with goals from Gilbert Alsop and Bill Sheppard. This is still regarded as one of the biggest upsets in Cup history as Arsenal were about to claim three straight League titles whereas Walsall were in Division Three (North).

WATFORD

Points: 15

Ground Name Vicarage Road
Capacity 21 577 (all seated)
Address Vicarage Road, Watford, WD18 0ER
Pitch Size 105 x 68.5 m
Nickname The Hornets/The Golden Boys/Yellow Army/The Horns/The 'Orns
Year Founded 1881
Website www.watfordfc.com

Watford's original nickname was 'The Brewers', in reference to the Benskins Brewery which owned Vicarage Road. They were then known as 'The Blues' until 1959, when a change of colours, to gold and black, and a vote by the supporters' club meant that 'The Hornets' was adopted.

WEST BROMWICH ALBION

Ground Name
The Hawthorns
Capacity 26 850 (all seated)
Address Halfords Lane, West Bromwich, West Midlands, B71 4LF
Pitch Size 105 x 68 m
Nickname Albion/The Baggies/WBA/West Brom
Year Founded 1878 (originally West Bromwich Strollers)
Website www.wba.co.uk

Albion have played their home games at the Hawthorns since 1900. At 551 ft (168 m) above sea level, the Hawthorns is the highest of all 92 Premier League and Football League grounds. The attendance record is 64 815 for an FA Cup sixth round tie with Arsenal in 1937. WBA legend Tony Brown holds the club record with 720 appearances between 1963–1981.

Points: 15

WEST HAM UNITED

Ground Name
Olympic Stadium – name to be confirmed 2016
Capacity 54 000 (all seated)
Address Olympic Park, Stratford, London E20 2ST
Pitch Size TBC
Nickname The Hammers/The Irons
Year Founded 1895 (originally Thames Ironworks)
Website www.whufc.com

When England beat West Germany 4-2 in the 1966 World Cup final at Wembley, captain Bobby Moore and both goalscorers, Martin Peters and Geoff Hurst – the only man to score a hat-trick in a World Cup final – were all Hammers players. In 2016 West Ham left The Boleyn Ground also known as Upton Park to move to the stadium originally built for the London 2012 Olympics. As well as football, the ground also holds regular athletic and other sporting events.

Points: 15

WIGAN ATHLETIC

Ground Name DW Stadium
Capacity 25 138 (all seated)
Address Loire Drive, Wigan, WN5 0UZ
Pitch Size 105 x 68 m
Nickname The Latics
Year Founded 1932
Website www.wiganlatics.co.uk

The club made headlines in 1995 when they signed the 'Three Amigos' – Roberto Martínez, Isidro Díaz and Jesús Seba. Martínez and Díaz were the first Spaniards to ever play in the FA Cup. They didn't win the Cup that year, but they did go on to win it in 2013 after a 1-0 win against Manchester City.

Points: 25

AFC WIMBLEDON

Ground Name The Cherry Red Records Stadium
Capacity 4 850 (2 265 seated)
Address Jack Goodchild Way, 422a Kingston Road, Kingston Upon Thames, KT1 3PB
Pitch Size 100.5 x 68.5 m
Nickname The Dons/The Wombles/ The Crazy Gang
Year Founded 2002
Website www.afcwimbledon.co.uk

When the FA allowed Wimbledon FC to relocate to Milton Keynes in 2002, supporters opposed to the move decided to form their own club, and AFC were born. Playing initially in the Combined Counties League, their average home attendance was higher than the exiled Wimbledon FC! Five promotions in nine seasons took the club to Football League status in 2011.

Points: 40 Top Spot

WOLVERHAMPTON WANDERERS

Ground Name
Molineux Stadium
Capacity 31 700
(all seated)
Address
Waterloo Road,
Wolverhampton,
WV1 4QR
Pitch Size 100 x 64 m
Nickname Wolves/The Wanderers
Year Founded 1877 (originally St. Luke's)
Website www.wolves.co.uk

Wolves' most successful period was in the 1950s when they won the League three times. Floodlights were installed at Molineux in 1953 and the club played a series of promotional friendlies. One match against Honved from Hungary was the first ever to be shown live on the BBC.

20 **Points: 20**

WYCOMBE WANDERERS

Ground Name
Adams Park
Capacity 10 284
Address
Hillbottom Road,
High Wycombe,
HP12 4HJ
Pitch Size
105 x 68.5 m
Nickname The Chairboys/The Blues
Year Founded 1887
Website
www.wycombewanderers.co.uk

Until 1990 the club played at Loakes Park which was famous for its twisting slope – this meant that when a player took a corner kick he could not see the diagonally opposite corner! The club's nickname recognises the town's long tradition of furniture making.

 Points: 40 Top Spot!

YEOVIL TOWN

Ground Name
Huish Park
Capacity 9 665
(5 212 seated)
Address Lufton
Way, Yeovil,
Somerset,
BA22 8YF
Pitch Size 105 x 66 m
Nickname The Glovers/Giant Killers
Year Founded 1895 (originally
Yeovil Casuals)
Website www.ytfc.net

Yeovil joined the League in 2003 but they were already famous for the sloping pitch at their former ground, and also for being the most successful non-league club in the FA Cup. Their greatest coup was in 1949 when they beat Sunderland and then faced Manchester United in the fifth round at Maine Road in front of more than 81 000 spectators. In January 2004, prior to their FA Cup third round tie with Liverpool, they released 'Yeovil True' that reached number 36 in the UK Singles Chart!

YORK CITY

Ground Name
Bootham
Crescent
Capacity 8 256
(3 409 seated)
Address York,
YO30 7AQ
Pitch Size
105 x 67.5 m
Nickname The Minstermen/Yorkies
Year Founded 1922
Website
www.yorkcityfootballclub.co.uk

The Minstermen spent most of their League career in the lower divisions and only recently returned to the League in 2012 after their relegation in 2004. A sponsorship deal with local employer, Nestlé, meant that for a number of years the stadium was renamed Kit Kat Crescent – just what you need for a half-time break!

45 Points: 45 **Top Spot!**

40 Points: 40 **Top Spot!**

5

Points: 5

WEMBLEY STADIUM

Capacity 90 000 (all seated)
Address Wembley, HA9 0WS
Pitch Size 105 x 68 m
Tenants England National Team
Year Founded 2007
Website www.wembleystadium.com

The original Empire Stadium with its famous Twin Towers was first used for the 1923 FA Cup final between Bolton and West Ham, when a crowd in excess of 200 000 crammed into the ground and overflowed on to the pitch. The current stadium was opened in 2007 and with a capacity of 90 000, it is the second largest stadium in Europe.

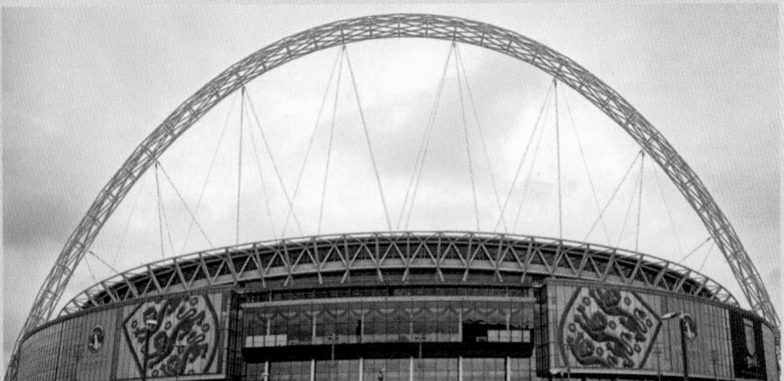

majeczka / shutterstock.com

10

Points: 10

HAMPDEN PARK

Capacity 52 063 (all seated)
Address Glasgow, G44 4QG
Pitch Size 105 x 68.5 m
Tenants Queen's Park F.C.
Year Founded 1903
Website www.hampdenpark.co.uk

There have been three Hampden Parks, and Queen's Park have used all three for their home ground. The current stadium was the biggest in the world when it opened in 1903, and at one stage it had a capacity of over 180 000. The ground is famous for the 'Hampden roar' created by the crowd to intimidate the opposition when Scotland are playing.

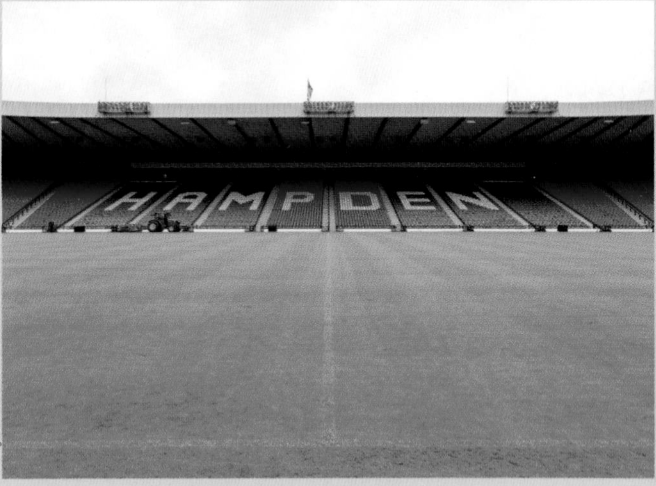

ATGImages / Shutterstock.com

PRINCIPALITY STADIUM

Points: 15

Capacity 74 500 (all seated)
Address Cardiff, CF10 1NS
Pitch Size 120 x 79 m
Tenants Football Association of Wales
Year Founded 1999
Website www.principalitystadium.wales

The stadium, with its retractable roof and a capacity of 74 500, was built to host the 1999 Rugby World Cup and it replaced the National Stadium which stood on the same site alongside the River Taff. It is officially the home of the Wales national rugby team but the football team plays the majority of its matches there also.

Deimos HP / shutterstock.com

Points: 15

ABERDEEN

Ground Name Pittodrie Stadium
Capacity 20 961 (all seated)
Address Pittodrie Street, Aberdeen, AB24 5QH
Pitch Size 100 x 66 m
Nickname The Dons/The Reds/The Dandies
Year Founded 1903
Website www.afc.co.uk

Under Alex Ferguson's guidance Aberdeen won three Scottish League titles and four Scottish Cups during the 1980s. But the greatest achievement of them all saw the Dons beat Real Madrid 2-1 to take the European Cup Winners' Cup in 1983.

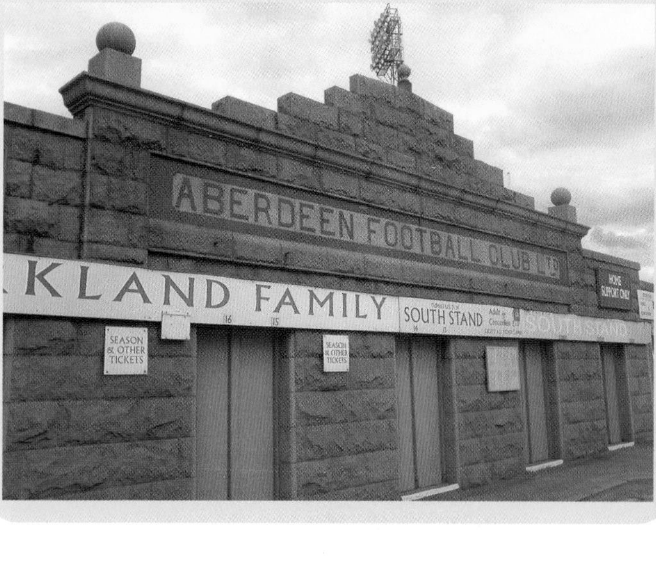

CELTIC

Ground Name Celtic Park
Capacity 60 832 (all seated)
Address 18 Kerrydale Street, Glasgow, G40 3RE
Pitch Size 105 x 68 m
Nickname The Bhoys/The Hoops/The Celts
Year Founded 1887
Website www.celticfc.net

Celtic have won countless honours in Scottish football but their finest prize was taken on 25 May 1967 when they became the first British team to win the European Cup, beating Internazionale 2-1 in Lisbon. The players became known as the 'Lisbon Lions' and were all born within 30 miles of Celtic Park.

Cornfields / shutterstock.com

DUNDEE

Ground Name
Dens Park
Capacity 11 850
(all seated)
Address
Sandeman
Street, Dundee,
DD3 7JY
Pitch Size 100 x 64 m
Nickname The Dees/The Dark Blues
Year Founded 1893
Website www.dundeefc.co.uk

Dundee were at their most successful during the 1960s, when in 1962, they won the Scottish Football League title. They also made it to the semi-finals of the European Cup in 1963 but were beaten 5-2 by AC Milan.

Points: 25

DUNDEE UNITED

Ground Name
Tannadice Park
Capacity 14 209
(all seated)
Address
Tannadice Street,
Dundee, DD3 7JW
Pitch Size 101 x 66 m
Nickname The Terrors/The Tangerines/The Arabs
Year Founded 1909 (originally Dundee Hibernian)
Website dufc.co

United have played at Tannadice Park since their formation in 1909. The ground is just 180 metres from Dens Park, the home of their city rivals Dundee. The two stadia are the closest of any senior grounds in the UK.

Points: 25

FALKIRK

Ground Name
Falkirk Stadium
Capacity 8750
(all seated)
Address
6 Stadium Way,
Falkirk, FK2 9EE
Pitch Size 100.5 x 65.5 m
Nickname The Bairns
Year Founded 1876
Website www.falkirkfc.co.uk

Falkirk is one of two clubs from the town, the other being East Stirlingshire. Their previous ground, Brockville Park, was responsible three times for them being denied promotion to the Scottish Premier League for not meeting the League standards at the time.

Points: 25

HAMILTON ACADEMICAL

Ground Name
New Douglas Park
Capacity 6078 (all seated)
Address Cadzow Avenue, Hamilton, ML3 0FT
Pitch Size 105 x 68.5 m
Nickname The Accies
Year Founded 1874
Website
www.hamiltonacciesfc.co.uk

The Accies are the only professional club in Britain to have originated from a school team, hence the name. Their best ever player was an Englishman, David Wilson, who scored 246 times for the club before his career was halted by the outbreak of World War II.

Points: 20

HEART OF MIDLOTHIAN

Ground Name Tynecastle Stadium
Capacity 17 420 (all seated)
Address Gorgie Road, Edinburgh, EH11 2NL
Pitch Size 98 x 67.5 m
Nickname The Maroons/Hearts/ The Jam Tarts/Jambos
Year Founded 1874
Website www.heartsfc.co.uk

The origin of the club's name is confusing. One theory links it to the Heart of Midlothian jail which was demolished in 1817, but gave its name to a local dance hall. The story then goes that some of the youths who attended the dance hall started to play football together and then founded the club.

Points: 15

HIBERNIAN

Ground Name Easter Road
Capacity 20 421 (all seated)
Address 12 Albion Place, Edinburgh, EH7 5QG
Pitch Size 102.5 x 67.5 m
Nickname Hibs/Hibees/The Cabbage
Year Founded 1875
Website www.hibernianfc.co.uk

Hibernian were the first British club to play in Europe after they were invited to take part in the inaugural season of the European Cup in 1955. They overcame Rot-Weiss Essen from West Germany and Swedish club Djurgårdens IF to reach the semi-finals, where they were defeated 3-0 on aggregate by Stade Reims from France.

Points: 15

INVERNESS CALEDONIAN THISTLE

Ground Name Tulloch Caledonian Stadium
Capacity 7800 (all seated)
Address Stadium Road, Inverness, IV1 1FF
Pitch Size 105 x 69 m
Nickname Caley Thistle/Caley Jags/ICT
Year Founded 1994
Website www.ictfc.com

Despite only being formed in 1994, the three teams from which Caley Thistle was formed were all founded in the late 1880s. Relegation from the Scottish Premier League in 2009 was a disappointment for them, however they came back fighting and were promoted into the top division again in 2010. Caley claimed their first Scottish Cup in 2015, beating Falkirk 2-1 at Hampden Park.

KILMARNOCK

Ground Name Rugby Park
Capacity 18 128 (all seated)
Address Kilmarnock, KA1 2DP
Pitch Size 102 x 68 m
Nickname Killie
Year Founded 1869
Website www.kilmarnockfc.co.uk

Killie took part in the first ever Scottish Cup in 1873 but lost 2-0 to Renton in the first round. Their greatest success, however, came in 1965, when a 2-0 win at Hearts on the final day of the season gave them the Scottish League title for the only time in the club's history.

Points: 35   **Top Spot!**

Points: 20

MOTHERWELL

Ground Name Fir
Park Stadium
Capacity 13 742
(all seated)
Address
Motherwell,
ML1 2QN
Pitch Size 100.5 x 67.5 m
Nickname The Well/The Steelmen
Year Founded 1886
Website www.motherwellfc.co.uk

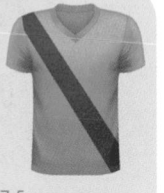

The Well's one and only Scottish
League title was claimed in 1931–32.
They scored 119 goals in the process
and Willie McFadyen's contribution
of 52 still stands as the record
number of goals for one player in a
Scottish season.

Points: 20

PARTICK THISTLE

Ground Name
Firhill Stadium
Capacity 13 079
(10 887 seated)
Address Firhill
Road, Glasgow,
G20 7AL
Pitch Size 105 x 69 m
Nickname Thistle/The Jags/The
Maryhill Magyars/The Harry Wraggs
Year Founded 1876
Website http://ptfc.co.uk/home

The Jags have had two great
achievements: winning the Scottish
Cup in 1921, and then the Scottish
League Cup in 1971. In this later
competition, they secured their
victory over Celtic against all odds,
winning 4-1 and scoring all four of
their goals during the first half.

Points: 25

Points: 10

Ground Name Ibrox Stadium
Capacity 50 987 (all seated)
Address 150 Edmiston Drive, Glasgow, G51 2XD
Pitch Size 105 x 69 m
Nickname The Gers/Teddy Bears/Blues
Year Founded 1872
Website www.rangers.co.uk

Rangers have won the Scottish League title on 54 occasions, a record for any team in any league in world football. The Ibrox stadium hosted the highest attendance for a league match in Britain when 118 567 watched the Rangers-Celtic 'Old Firm' derby on 2 January 1939. From 1872 until 2012 Rangers had always played in the top tier of Scottish football, but financial turmoil led to the club being liquidated at the end of the 2011–12 season. The club under a new organisation was admitted into Scottish League Two for the start of the next season and then three promotions in the next four years, saw Rangers return to the Scottish Premiership at the end of the 2015–2016 season.

ROSS COUNTY

Ground Name Victoria Park/ Global Energy Stadium
Capacity 6541 (all seated)
Address Jubilee Road, Dingwall, IV15 9QZ
Pitch Size 91 x 69 m
Nickname The Staggies
Year Founded: 1929
Website www.rosscountyfootballclub.co.uk

Having won the Challenge Cup twice, and also the Scottish First Division, Second Division and Third Division, Ross County were promoted to the Scottish Premier League in 2012. They have earned the nickname 'The Staggies' on account of the stag's head that appears on their badge. In 2016, a last-minute goal secured a 2-1 victory for the Staggies over Hibernian in the Scottish League Cup final, clinching the first major trophy in the club's history.

Points: 35 Top Spot!

ST JOHNSTONE

Ground Name McDiarmid Park
Capacity 10 673 (all seated)
Address Crieff Road, Perth, PH1 2SJ
Pitch Size 105 x 68.5 m
Nickname The Saints
Year Founded 1884
Website www.perthstjohnstonefc.co.uk

After winning the 2008–09 Scottish League First Division, The Saints were promoted to the Scottish Premiership. McDiarmid Park, which opened in 1989 after the move from Muirton Park, was the first purpose-built all-seater stadium in the United Kingdom.

Points: 25

INDEX

i-SPY

How to get your i-SPY certificate and badge

Let us know when you've become a super-spotter with 1000 points and we'll send you a special certificate and badge!

HERE'S WHAT TO DO!

✓ Ask an adult to check your score.

✓ Visit www.collins.co.uk/i-SPY to apply for your certificate. If you are under the age of 13 you will need a parent or guardian to do this.

✓ We'll send your certificate via email and you'll receive a brilliant badge through the post!